GET A RING ON IT

10 Secrets To
Becoming Wife Material

by Lasana Smith, MCM

Praise for Lasana Smith's

Get A Ring On It:
10 Secrets To Becoming Wife Material

"A great guide for *single women* seeking the love-relationship that leads to marriage. *Get a Ring On It*, provides every reader with insight that forces them to take a step back and look not only within themselves, but also outside of themselves and ask the question out loud, "*Am I wife material?*" As a relationship coach, I work with many couples and individuals that have trouble maintaining their relationships and marriages. The principles and roles of husband, wife, mother, father, friend, and lover are expected to be fulfilled and it is assumed that they will be fulfilled without prior discussion or exploration of what these roles signify in their relationship. This book gives women the first steps toward a relationship that leads to marriage. The conversation you have with *yourself* about being someone's wife and the roles *you* take on as a wife. These are the preliminary steps toward the road to

becoming a wife while choosing, and being chosen by a man worthy of being your husband and partner through life. *Are you ready?* Well, you will know after you read, *Get A Ring On It!*"
~ Sophie Lherisse, Life & Relationship Coach-Expert, *EDEN* Life Coaching Services

"Get a Ring On It delves deep into the key areas where most women struggle without even knowing it - exposing secrets most men don't even talk about. If you are hitting a wall in finding "The One", this book is a must-read for anyone serious about settling down with Mr. Right."
~ Robinne Burrell, Director of Mobile, Match.com

"This book is absolutely AMAZING!!! So many truths, and much needed. I feel like you really tapped into something with this book. I completely agree with every point. Great job of weaving in personal and public stories and facts with real life concepts."
~ Nikki Faye, Co-founder of *MixandMatchLA.com* and Matchmaker

"I love this book. Seriously, if you're a woman who wants it all: the house, the husband, and the kids this book is for you. The days of asking, "What is he thinking?" are over. I can't wait to get everyone in my book club to read it so we can discuss these secrets even more."
~Adrienne Sivad, Director of *Itty Bitty Events* Planning Company

This book is dedicated to my parents who have always encouraged me and who have shown me the true meaning of love.

Girl Power-

A portion of the proceeds from the sale of this book will be donated to "Girl Up!"

"Girl Up" is an innovative campaign of the United Nations Foundation that envisions a world where all girls around the world, have the opportunity to become educated, healthy, safe, counted and positioned to be the next generation of leaders.

www.girlup.org

Acknowledgements

There are a few people I would like to thank for assisting me in bringing this book to the world:

- Thank you to my business coach and partner, Natasha Allrich who always believed I had books inside of me, and encouraged me to write them.
- Thank you William Gordon for creating the most beautiful and amazing book cover.
- Thank you Khadijah Ali-Coleman and Joyce Kennedy for your invaluable feedback and notes.
- Thank you Ashannti Hill for creating my effective press releases and La'Tanya Martin for your assistance with my public relations.
- Thank you Lieutenant Christopher Washington, Denzil Wilson and Lee Sebastiany for giving me your male stamp of approval on these ten secrets.
- Thank you Adrienne Davis, Sophie Lherisse, Robinne Burrell, Janet Casamento, Faye

Tillery, Allison Miller and Cristina Torres for placing your female stamp of approval on this book.

- Thank you Bhavisha Patel, Tristan Borden, Maxine Tull, Timothy Conley, Daniel Atwater, Peter Osbourne, Rahiem Grimsley, Jerry Dufreny, Renee and Darrell Thomas, and each of the men and women who were personally interviewed by me or participated in my all female and all male focus groups. Thank you for being so candid and transparent with me.
- Thank you Mathew Curtis for your encouragement and support.

GET A RING ON IT
10 Secrets To Becoming Wife Material

Secret #1: Be Wife-Minded

Secret #2: Be a Quality Woman

Secret #3: Be Loving

Secret #4: Be Down To Earth

Secret #5: Be Active

Secret #6: Be Inter-Dependent

Secret #7: Be Compatible

Secret #8: Be Jekyll and Hyde

Secret #9: Be a Good Money Manager

Secret #10: Be Supportive

Introduction

It happened again. I stared at the white envelope with my name written in bright blue calligraphy. I instantly knew what was inside. As I slid out the embroidered stationary from within, I recognized the familiar line, "request the honor of your presence as they exchange their wedding vows," another wedding invitation. It was my fifth one for the year. And this invitation was really only a formality since I was a bridesmaid. The second time for the year I would be wearing a beautifully styled dress walking down the aisle…but not as a bride.

With the exception of my aunt and uncle, I never saw a healthy marital relationship growing up. Married for over 35 years, my aunt and uncle met in elementary school in Barbados, West Indies. He revealed his affection by teasing her when the teacher put him in charge of the class. Over time, she also developed feelings for him. When my grandmother realized their little crush, she transferred my aunt to a school on the other side of the island. As she believed my aunt was too young for a boyfriend. She wanted her to focus on her education. However instead of ending their love affair, this separation fueled it. They would send letters to each other and have secret meetings once a month at places such as the library. Their love even transcended her move from Barbados at 18 to New York City. A year and a half later they were engaged and their marriage has survived the transitions of having three children, gaining higher education and creating a sound financial legacy for their family.

I would spend summers with them as a child and never saw them argue or disrespect one another. Rather I saw them always being loving and supportive of each other and looking out for each other's needs. That's how I still believe a marriage should be.

Conversely, I grew up in a single parent household with a fiercely independent mother who played the role of both mother and father. She was never dependent on a man for anything and prided herself in taking care of our family's needs. She taught me, as so many women are taught today, to get an education so I could secure a good job and take care of myself. That way, I would be independent and wouldn't have to depend on a man to take care of me.

My upbringing led my primary focus to being more about pursuing my dream career than pursuing my dream husband. Although it was always my personal desire to be married, I believed one day it would just happen. Somewhere along the journey of going to school and working, he would appear. We would fall in love and would live happily ever after.

In reality, uniting with my ideal life partner proved to be more challenging than initially anticipated. Although I dated quality men who may have considered marrying me, it became evident over time a marriage to any of them would not have been fulfilling or sustaining. I would only have been married for the sake of being married. However it was never my desire to simply wear a wedding ring. It was more important to me to have a marriage that would be of substance, a commitment that would endure "til death did us part."

There were times when I seriously dated someone and thought to myself, "This might be it, he might be 'the one'" and was disappointed each time I was proven wrong. The man would say something like, "I care about you but I'm just not ready to settle down yet." Or "You're a good girl and I don't want to taint that," and soon after the relationship would come to an end.

I watched disappointingly as time went on and these men married other women. In addition, my girlfriends were getting married left and right. As happy as I was for them, I would find myself in the bathroom at their weddings crying about where my love life was going. Wondering when it would be my turn.

That's when I made the decision to take responsibility and change the direction of my love life. I refused to allow my destiny to be, "always the bridesmaid and never the bride." What did my married girlfriends know that I didn't? What were my ex-boyfriends and male friends not telling me? I decided to make it my personal mission to uncover the secrets of what made a woman, "wife material."

At first I took the informal approach. Asking my married girlfriends and male friends to share any tips that would assist me in going from a great girlfriend, to someone a man would decide to turn into a great wife. This proved challenging as many men didn't want to break the "guy code." They would give me vague answers like, "every man is different" or "that would take awhile to answer."

On the other hand, many of my married girlfriends didn't even know what they did to be considered wife material. If they had any sort of idea they would always say something like, "Give me a call later and we'll talk about it." Except between taking care of their husband, kids, career and themselves, they never actually found the time to discuss the topic.

Finally I was given an opportunity to learn once and for all what men determined as, "wife material." Observing all male focus groups, men candidly answered relationship questions. This allowed me to gain a clear understanding of what characteristics they looked for while dating, to decide if a woman was the one they would ask to become their wife.

After countless observations, conversations and through personal experiences and insights, I finally uncovered the secrets. The only thing now was to determine what would be done with them? Would I simply keep these suppressed revelations to myself? Become married and like my married girlfriends, then become too busy to share them? Thus continuing to keep this information hidden from other single women who so desperately wanted to know what they could do to change the direction of their love lives? Or would I break the code of silence and share these secrets helping single women everywhere understand how to become wife material? I decided to do the latter and share the findings I learned throughout this book.

As my male friends established, I quickly realized one man might not as strongly cherish the attributes that another man may value in a wife. However, I also learned there were a few characteristics overall men looked for in a wife regardless of race, religion or age. These qualities became the ten secrets that will be uncovered within the following chapters. At the end of each chapter are, "Wife Material Lessons" and "Reflections" to further share how you can apply the insights from each of the ten secrets to your own personal life. It is my intention after you finish reading this book, you will have a firm grasp on which behaviors you may want to enhance, modify or add to your lifestyle and dating practices in order to transition from being single to wife material.

Learning and practicing these secrets will help you to do more than just *Get A Ring On It*. These secrets will allow you to improve yourself as an individual. As you become more desirable, you will attract better quality men into your life that will recognize your value and worth. In a time of increasing divorce rates and decreasing marriage rates, it will give you the essential tools to attract a loving husband and create a harmonious, sustaining marriage.

I am looking forward to hearing your success stories so please email them to me at lasanaonline@gmail.com.

* Note: Throughout this book, the names have been changed to provide you juicy insights, candid quotes and real-life examples without revealing the identities of those interviewed.

Prelude: Get A Ring On It

"Do not bring people in your life who weigh you down. And trust your instincts ... good relationships feel good. They feel right. They don't hurt. They're not painful. That's not just with somebody you want to marry, but it's with the friends that you choose. It's with the people you surround yourselves with."

~ Michelle Obama

Prelude: Get A Ring On It

The secrets about to be revealed in the following chapters will give you direct insight into the mind of men and what they are looking for in a wife. Yet you may feel empowered to know within my findings, it is apparent that a man's primary motivation to make money and achieve considerable success is to impress, love and provide for a woman and ultimately a family. A man's aspiration to appear great in the eyes of a woman is what has led to his achievements from pre-historic times through today. Therefore as a woman it is important to know, you have the ability to determine the progression of romantic partnerships in your life. Consciously decide who to date. Then advance only at a pace that feels comfortable.

Do not let a desire to be married block your view of potential relationship issues and red flags. Ultimately, even after becoming a woman of wife material, it is necessary for both individuals to be in tune and flow through the process of dating to marriage. Each partner has to be the right person at the right time. So have a vision of what you want in a husband and marital relationship and hold fast to these dreams, values and ideals. Believe in your ability to attract the right mate and one day soon, you will *Get A Ring On It*.

Secret #1
Be Wife-Minded

"When you realize you want to spend the rest of your life with somebody, you want the rest of your life to start as soon as possible."

~Nora Ephron, *When Harry Met Sally*

Be Wife-Minded

Four years ago, my college friend Bethany, decided to make some changes in her life. She saw herself approaching 30 without being married or having children and wanted to make that transition. She decided to take an overall assessment of her life and evaluate how she could become her best self. If she was a guy what qualities would make her, ask herself for her number? After taking inventory of the changes she felt were necessary, Bethany chose to implement them by working out, taking care of her skin, and wearing clothes that made her look and feel exceptional.

She also created a list of what she was looking for in a potential mate. Focusing on what was important to her; she envisioned the values, ideals and physical characteristics she wanted to find in her ideal husband. She determined her deal breakers, which behaviors she would and would not accept and which ones she could compromise. "There's no reason why I can't find someone I want to marry," she said to herself and went out on dates in search of her best match. She knew it would be a journey, but she refused to take "no" for an answer and trusted her intuition.

In order to make sure her judgment would not be impaired, she gave up alcohol during this dating period. "I didn't want alcohol to induce or drive my emotions," Bethany confided in me, "I wanted my attractions to be pure." For the same reasons, she also decided she would not have sex with a man to whom she was not exclusive. Bethany believed if she wanted something different, she would have to behave differently.

Bethany judged the potential of each man she dated. She had a 3 date maximum and categorized each one as: (1) "Good guy and I would like to see again to see where it goes." (2) "Good guy but I'm not attracted to him." (3) "Good guy but he's not ready for long term commitment." Her dating pool began to shrink as her standards heightened. She no longer accepted "booty call," calls after midnight or other behaviors from men she felt were disrespectful. Bethany stood on her deal breakers and would not compromise what she wanted simply to be in a relationship. In addition, Bethany gave herself a time limit for how long she wanted to date a man before she was engaged…six months.

"I believe in love," Bethany told herself repeatedly during this process knowing she would soon attract her ideal match. She was even open to moving to another city or country so she could meet him. A year later she finally made a connection through a dating website. Although she lived in Atlanta, her dream man flew in from Chicago to spend time with her. After a six month long distance courtship they became engaged, are now happily married and living together. "It's so nice to find someone who loves me unconditionally," Bethany exclaims smiling from ear to ear, "I'm so lucky to have him." Bethany took ownership and control of her romantic situation. She allowed for no excuses. Instead she evaluated herself and what she desired in a husband to create the love she wanted in her life.

Many single women do just the opposite. They don't make being married a priority. It's just another item on their checklist. They devote more of their time and energy to their education, careers and personal lives. Then wonder later why they aren't yet married. I now realize the women who get married are the ones who decide to be married. They take the necessary steps to make marriage a priority in their lives.

Wife-minded women create the space for marriage by taking on wifely characteristics even before they officially have a ring. They shift their mindset in who they date and how they think. The wife-minded woman primarily dates only men who are looking to be in a committed relationship and who want to marry. She prefers to date men who are established professionally and financially knowing these types of men are more confident, stable and the most likely candidates to progress into a marriage. Men who are already married, in another committed relationship or have other types of emotional or physical baggage such as "baby mama drama" are seen as time-wasters for the wife-minded woman. Instead, she quickly considers more suitable mates.

Once she meets a man she considers to be marriage material, she is very outspoken regarding her desire to be married. Sometimes she shares this aspiration in the beginning of the relationship. On the other hand, she may wait until after the relationship has progressed to when she feels it is ready to advance to the next level. Either way, understanding most men don't pick-up on subtle hints or clues, she is forthcoming. Her ability to communicate this desire is what puts her ahead of many single women who feel uneasy approaching the subject of marriage, or wait for the man to initiate the conversation.

Although the wife-minded woman is very upfront about her desire to be married, she also has noticeable ways of showing the man she is dating that she is the right choice to be his wife. One such way is she looks out for his needs. An example is a woman who is willing to watch the action movie her boyfriend wants to see instead of the romantic comedy she may really want to watch because she knows it will make him happy. Or the woman who suggests her boyfriend bring his coat as it might get cold later. She shifts from a self-centered view of the world to a view that looks out for his needs as well as her own.

As most men still appreciate tradition, the wife-minded woman is open to focusing time in traditionally feminine roles such as cooking, cleaning and laundry. Keep in mind these may not become her primary duties nor may she be the best at any of these activities. However she realizes that putting in effort in these areas will allow her man to feel nurtured.

Wife Material Lesson

To be a wife-minded woman you must make becoming married a priority in your life. Evaluate where you are and what you bring to the table. Also determine what you want in a potential husband. Then begin to take on wifely characteristics even before you are married. Only date men who are looking to be in a committed relationship and who want to marry. This will prevent you from dating men who are unavailable, or not looking for anything serious. Once you meet the man who matches that of your ideal partner, you must communicate to him your desire to be married. Become confident enough to make sure your needs are being met. However, become selfless enough to also look out for the needs of your partner. Consider taking on some of the traditionally feminine roles. Having roles in your relationship will make it easier for you and your partner to know what each can contribute to the household. Being able to turn a house into a home will assure a man you are the one with whom he wants to spend the rest of his life.

Reflections #1

1. Is marriage a priority for you? If so, what actions are you taking to reflect that?

2. Are you currently your best self? If not, what qualities or behaviors can you change or improve starting today?

3. What attributes can you bring into a marriage? List them.

4. What attributes are you looking for in a potential husband? List values, ideas, physical characteristics, etc.

5. What are your relationship deal breakers? What are you not willing to accept and where are you willing to compromise?

Secret #2
Be a Quality Woman

"I chose my wife, as she did her wedding gown, for qualities that would wear well."

~ Oliver Goldsmith

Be a Quality Woman

While growing up, my dad would tell me, "It's not looks that differentiate women. Looks are important, yes, but over time those fade. What is really important to a man? The type of woman she is. Does she have an education? Can he walk down the street without every man thinking to himself he had a piece of her? Can she be the mother of his children?"

If a single woman wants a man to be attracted to her on a deeper level, the level where he can think of her as wife material, she has to be a quality woman. It is essential she displays characteristics such as uniqueness, passion for causes and a consciousness of the world. Thus he can get a hold of her overall value. She also needs to value herself and display her intelligence so he can see her as someone with whom he can have meaningful intimacy.

Men do not enter into committed relationships that could lead to marriage lightly. They see it as a risk-taking venture. One of the main reasons for this perspective is because they see dating as a serious financial expense. While being interviewed, 27 year-old Don, a frequent dater who would like to be married by 30 once described dating as, "when money comes out of your pocket." He also revealed that he determined the type of dates he took a female on by where his finances were before the date, "after pay day, it could be an expensive dinner. Before pay day, it would be something less expensive such as a walk along the beach."

Accordingly, men feel the opportunity cost of purchasing flowers, buying dinner, paying for movies and sweeping a girl off her feet are high and not worth the risk unless a woman can reveal how she is different from other available women. Once he is able to recognize her uniqueness, he will start treating her differently by paying attention and showing he cares about her. As his respect level for her rises, so does his desire to spend more time with her. This creates the desire within him to make the relationship exclusive setting the stage for engagement and marriage.

Men are not willing to invest their time and energy into a relationship when they do not feel they can respect the woman they are dating. They have to be able to trust the woman especially when it comes to fidelity. If a man does not feel his partner will be faithful to him when times are good and bad, he will not marry her.

In addition, even though every man is different when it comes to how he perceives a woman's sexual history. One thing men care more about than the quantity of partners she's had is the quality of the men with whom she had sex. During a personal phone conversation, Jon, a 30 year-old single engineer looking to attract his wife revealed to me, "When I find out a woman slept with a man who's less deserving of her than me, it makes me scratch her off my list." Constantly having sex outside of committed relationships, and sleeping with men who are not at a similar social status or above are also major turn-offs for men. The appearance of promiscuity will prevent a man from seeing a woman as wife-material.

Unless a man is looking for a trophy wife, he is more concerned about her character than her cup size. The woman he marries has to be someone he feels comfortable introducing to his family and his friends. She must be someone he could envision being the mother of his children.

Wife Material Lesson

Becoming a woman of wife material means you emerge as a woman of quality. By valuing yourself, you reflect your value to your partner. Share your uniqueness, passions and intelligence with him.

Become trustworthy, respectable and sexually discerning. Displaying these qualities will allow your partner to see his future in your eyes. It will also let him be comfortable discussing his life goals and aspirations with you in hopes you will want to be a part of them. Once he determines you are the woman he wants to spend the rest of his life with, he will ask you to marry him.

Reflections #2

1. What characteristics such as uniqueness, passion for causes, and a consciousness of the world do you feel you possess?
2. What qualities do you possess that sets you apart from other women?
3. Do people consider you trustworthy? If not, how can you improve your trustworthiness?
4. Are you faithful in relationships? How do you define fidelity vs. infidelity?
5. Are you sexually discerning? If not, what changes can you make today to become more discerning of your sexual partners?

Secret #3
Be Loving

"A successful marriage requires falling in love many times, always with the same person."

~Mignon McLaughlin

Be Loving

When my best friend Rachel was getting married, her 26 year-old, soon-to-be groom, Derrick, was asked at their engagement party why he selected her to be his wife. His response was, "She loves me so much. I didn't think I would ever find someone who would love me as much as she does." His comment struck a chord, lingering in the back of my mind. He didn't say he was marrying her because she was the most beautiful woman he ever met or because she had the best body he had ever seen. No. He was marrying her because she was the most loving woman he had ever dated.

Men want to marry women who love them. Women who show them loving acts of kindness and thoughtfulness are the ones who they choose to take relationships with more seriously. Picture the first woman with whom most men have any interaction. It is their mother. Who is more loving, gentle, sweet, kind and thoughtful than a mother? As boys grow into men, they look for women who can replicate this loving figure in their lives.

Initially, a man is not able to tell right away how loving a woman will be so he looks for clues: Does she smile often? Is she playful? Does she like when he touches her? When a man can say, "yes" to these questions, the woman starts to peak his interest more. Then he looks for the woman to show she loves him in deeper ways. It could be making him dinner. Or ordering in food and having it ready for him once he comes home from a long day of work. Picking up his medication and taking his temperature if he is sick. Even simply giving him a massage on a sore back after an intense work out shows a man he is being cared for and loved.

But what about when a man makes his partner upset, does he still expect her to show him love then? Yes. A woman who truly loves a man will still find ways even while arguing to show love. She will try to fight fairly and practice not throwing personal shots at him. She will attempt not to go to bed angry, as she will try to resolve their disagreement beforehand. In marriage it rings true there will be challenges. I have seen examples of married couples when there was a time the wife did not feel her husband was worthy and deserving of her love. Maybe he made a major decision without consulting her, was dishonest about a personal situation, or worst yet unfaithful to her in their marriage. But the amazing thing I discovered was regardless of these mistakes; underneath it all, the wife still loved him. That kind of love is what truly holds marriages together. A man realizes this from the beginning. So he is looking for a woman to show him she is capable of giving him a love that is concrete. A love that is unconditional.

However a woman doesn't have to wait until she has a partner to practice being loving, she should first practice being loving to herself. How can she truly love someone else if she doesn't love herself first? A woman of wife material will book a spa day, enjoy a manicure and pedicure and even send herself flowers so she can show herself love. It's in loving herself that she gains self-confidence and a feeling of self-worth. Both are attributes men find attractive. In loving herself, she creates a space for others, including her future husband, to also love her.

Wife Material Lesson

As a woman of wife material it is important for you to become loving. As your partnership with your ideal mate grows, show him you care about him throughout the relationship by displaying loving acts of kindness. You practice showing love. Even through times of discord such as during an argument. Keep in mind that being loving starts with loving yourself. It is only after you love yourself that you truly have the ability to love another. Uncover ways you can show yourself devotion. The more loved you feel the more you will attract love and once you attract love you will be able to return it. Thus is the circle of love.

Reflections #3

1. What activities do you do on a daily, weekly and monthly basis to show yourself love?
2. How often do you smile? Are you playful? Affectionate?
3. How do you show loving acts of kindness?
4. Are you able to "fight fairly" when arguing? How can you find compassion even when there is discord?
5. In what ways can you become more loving than you are now?

Secret #4
Be Down To Earth

"Success in marriage does not come merely through finding the right mate, but through being the right mate."

~Barnett R. Brickner

Be Down To Earth

"French Fries" is how 35 year-old Lee describes the women he commonly sees on line outside of the club. During an entirely male focus group on relationships, the former pro-athlete who is actively seeking to attract his life partner and now works as a bouncer at a popular Hollywood nightclub further explained, "They are all trying to fulfill the model stereotype. They dress the same, smell the same and look the same. It's like they all just stepped off the set of the latest music video."

I always notice on the days I dress down, I get more attention. Let me explain to you what my version of dressed down is: jogging suit or sweats, hair in a ponytail or under a hat and little to no make-up. Yet somehow, I seem to get more attention from men on the days I dress like this than on the days I look like a glamour girl. "What gives?" I asked my male friends.

"Listen," they explained to me, "on the days you dress down is when you look the most natural and approachable. It makes you appear comfortable in your own skin and confident. When a woman looks too made up, she intimidates us. It brings out our insecurities. We don't ask her out because it brings back memories of the pretty girls who turned us down or snubbed us in the past. It also makes us wonder what she would look like in the morning without all the make-up, jewelry and hair. When you are dressed down, you appear more down to earth."

Further on this topic, Lee continued, "If I see a woman who is very attractive or has an attractive physical body part, dating isn't the first thing on my mind."

Men see many women every day: school, work, and while grocery shopping amongst other places. Some of these women are beautiful, but it's usually not the most beautiful women they marry. That's because they don't consider a woman as wife material if she looks and acts like every other woman. They are looking for the woman who stands out. They are looking for women with personalities who come across as individuals. Selfish, conceited, materialistic, needy and insecure women need not apply for the role as a man's life partner. Men want to be with a woman whom they can feel comfortable being themselves.

Most of the time, men are simply dressed in a baseball cap, t-shirt, jeans/shorts and sneakers or flip-flops. A woman who is constantly wearing mini dresses and high heels may be a great fling, but she rarely is seen as wife material. This is because a man knows during the majority of the marriage the woman will not be dressed up. Therefore a man will not feel comfortable committing to a woman unless he knows he will still be attracted to her even when she is completely natural.

I have heard many single women say, "I don't wear these hair extensions, extravagant jewelry or expensive/sexy clothing for him, I do it for myself. It makes me feel beautiful." That's a fine attitude to have if a woman wants to date casually or remain single for the rest of her life but if she is looking to become wife material, she has to tone it down. Appear and be more down to earth.

The reason being down to earth is even more important is because most men are raised by society to be the providers. They recognize the lifestyle this woman has grown accustomed to having before them, will be the one she will expect them to maintain after they marry. Men, including wealthy ones, do not desire to spend the majority of their money on a woman's hair appointments and beauty regime. If they do it, they would prefer it to be out of choice but not because they are feeling pressured. Men will become reluctant to explore the long-term potential of a relationship with a high maintenance woman if they feel it is going to waste their money or their time.

Being down to earth doesn't just affect a woman's appearance and clothing; it also affects how she reacts on their dates and her overall approach to life. A man wants to see how spontaneous and open-minded a woman can be. Men like to sweat and get dirty. He wants to know if the woman he's dating is willing to do activities that make her sweat and get dirty too. There may also be times he just wants to go for fast food or make dinner at home instead of dining out. If she complains, she comes off like a princess but if she's genuinely enjoying herself and having a good time, she is seen as a woman with whom he would like to spend more time. He views her as someone with whom he can imagine himself building a future.

Wife Material Lesson

As a woman of wife material you become down to earth. You can display this in several ways: dressing casually with less make-up, being open-minded and being spontaneous. Of course, you can still dress up for formal events and other times you feel desirable, but your dress should tend to resemble that of your partner. This is especially important since men like to be spontaneous. Become a woman who can change her outfit at a moment's notice quickly, if or when plans change. This way you are always prepared when he wants you to participate in activities with him. It also lets him feel comfortable and at ease. This gives him the ability to be himself around you allowing him to view you as long-term potential.

Reflections #4

1. How does your current appearance display your uniqueness?

2. What changes can you make in your appearance to display you are down to earth and approachable?

3. What are the aspects of your appearance that may need to be toned down or removed to display you are down to earth?

4. Are you open-minded? If not, how can you see yourself becoming more open-minded?

5. How do you handle spontaneity? How do you feel being more spontaneous could improve your life?

Secret #5
Be Active

"A woman worries about the future until she gets a husband, while a man never worries about the future until he gets a wife."

~ Charles M Schwab

Be Active

When Carrie Bradshaw, the lead character in the hit cable series, Sex and the City, shared with her friends her desire to reunite with her ex-boyfriend, Aidan, they urged her to take the safe approach by getting online and emailing him. However being an old-fashioned girl, Carrie didn't believe in email. She preferred to call her ex several times and hang up before he answered the phone. Encouraging her to get online, her best friend Miranda explained to her that she could also use the Internet for online shopping. "No, shopping is my cardio." Carrie exclaimed.

How many women, like Carrie, can relate to shopping being their form of exercise?

Men like being physically active and exercising. Therefore when a man is looking for a wife, he wants to be with someone who will be active with him and accompany him during activities such as walks, bike rides and rock climbing. Being active shows a man the woman cares about her health. The healthiness of a woman is important to a man because not only does it increases the likelihood she will live longer providing him long-term companionship, but it also increases the likelihood she will be healthy enough to be sexually active and bear his children if he would like to have a family. Her healthiness allows him to feel more confident in her ability to become a mother one day.

An active woman will also motivate her partner to be more active. While single, men tend to be very active. Going to the gym, jogging and playing basketball with their friends come very naturally for them. However a fear of theirs is when they get married they will become too busy to do these things and become too comfortable or lazy. They have seen their male friends gain the "married 15 pounds" and don't want that to happen to them. A woman who is active will give a man confidence he will have a partner to encourage him to work out, stay active, and lessen his chances of becoming overweight.

An active woman will also assure her partner she will be more likely to maintain her weight after she is married. This is a very sensitive subject for both men and women. Women want to feel comfortable knowing their mate will love them unconditionally no matter what their size. However, men being visual by nature can lose attraction to their wives if they gain too much weight after marriage.

"I know this sounds wrong to say, but after my wife gained 10 pounds, I just lost physical attraction to her. I didn't feel intimate toward her anymore. It was like we were just roommates," disclosed Nate, a 32 year-old divorced medical doctor who would one day like to re-marry.

Additionally, active doesn't just mean exercise. When a man thinks about an active woman, he also thinks of her having an active social life. A woman's willingness to actively give to herself and others can be displayed by: volunteering in meaningful community organizations, being involved in church, temple, mosque or other spiritual activities, and engaging in hobbies she enjoys. A woman who has a more active social life is viewed as more confident, independent and rings more a feeling of self-worth. She also gives her partner the space he needs to live his life. Accordingly, it releases the pressure of him feeling responsible to constantly entertain and manage her desires, allowing him to see her as having long-term potential.

Wife Material Lesson

As a woman of wife material you find ways to become active. Do physical activity such as exercise so you can be healthy. Encourage your partner to do the same. You also create and maintain an active social life that displays your confidence and self-worth. This allows you to have some independence while in the relationship, and gives your partner the space he needs to have some as well. Being an active woman will show your partner you are the type of woman who has long-term potential. A woman he can see himself being with and creating a family.

Reflections #5

1. What forms of exercise or physical activity keep you active?
2. What forms of exercise or physical activity can you envision yourself doing with your partner?
3. What are your hobbies?
4. What organizations do you devote time to or volunteer?
5. In what ways could you create a more physically and socially active lifestyle than you have now?

Secret #6
Be Inter-Dependent

"After marriage, husband and wife become two sides of a coin; they just can't face each other, but still they stay together."

~ Al Gore

Be Inter-Dependent

The woman's liberation movement may have done a lot for the advancement of women in their professional lives, but it may have really set women back in their romantic lives. In the 1970s, Gloria Steinem once said, "We're becoming the men we wanted to marry." As a result 31 year-old married military lieutenant, Lavon, shared a statement during a private discussion on relationships which resonated with me, "So many women are so busy being good men; they don't know how to attract good men." Ouch.

There is a new trend slowly impacting romantic relationships as we know it. A societal shift so monumental, it is changing the way women and men relate to each other. Gender roles now cease to exist, as women are more likely to graduate from college, maintain their jobs and are increasingly becoming the breadwinners of their households. Conversely, the Fox reality channel featured a reality series entitled, "Househusbands of Hollywood." What's going on? Are women becoming the new men?

The Women's Liberation Movement impacted the roles of women in the 20th and 21st centuries. What began as a movement to eliminate gender inequality in our laws and culture soon became a complete transformation of gender roles as women were taught to be independent and strong. Women could do anything a man could do, possibly even better than they could. But where did these beliefs place men? How did these changes affect single women who wanted to marry?

It seems men and women are now totally confused. Should a man open the car door for a woman? Who pays for the date? What if the woman makes more money than the man?

Men in this day and age are used to women being independent. They have come to embrace it and many men even appreciate having a woman as a partner to assist in splitting the cost of living expenses. However society still teaches men to be the overall providers for their family, to have a good job and secure finances. So when a woman comes to a man already with her own home, high paying job and financial savings in order, it intimidates the average man. Where does he fit into her life? How can he provide for her? She comes off as too independent, too self-reliant. The opposite of this is also true. If a woman has no job, no savings and just spends her entire day at home watching television, a man sees her as a dependent. And a man is not looking for any dependents unless he has children.

What a man is looking for in a woman he considers as wife material is a woman who is inter-dependent. This is a woman who is independent enough to be his partner, but dependent enough to allow him to still be an integral part of their household. Essentially at times this woman leads and other times she allows her partner to be the guide.

"If a woman really wants to keep her man, she should spend more time stroking his ego than she does stroking his [privates]," declared 40 year-old eligible bachelor and photographer Rahman. That's because a man wants to feel wanted. He also wants a woman who respects him. A woman who is independent enough to have a fulfilling life of her own while also allowing him to feel like he's an important part of her life. This inter-dependence releases the pressure of a man from feeling smothered, yet creates a space and a need in her life that only he can fill. It is an inter-dependent woman a man is looking to marry.

Wife Material Lesson

As a woman of wife material you learn how to become inter-dependent. You can do this by being an independent woman who has a fulfilling life, yet shows her partner her dependence towards the relationship by creating space and time for him. Your words and actions provide your partner a feeling of being wanted and respected. Therefore, you become the type of woman who successfully manages the balancing act of being in control of your own life, while allowing him to feel like he's still an integral part of it. As a result you will attract a man who wants to commit to you for life.

Reflections #6

1. Do you feel we have gender roles in our society in regards to dating and marriage? If so, do you believe we should? Which ones are most important to you?
2. If you are currently in a relationship, how do you show your partner he is wanted and respected?
3. In what ways do you display your independence in romantic relationships?
4. In what ways do you display your dependence in romantic relationships?
5. How will you combine the above to display your inter-dependence in romantic relationships?

Secret #7
Be Compatible

"People shop for a bathing suit with more care than they do a husband or wife. The rules are the same. Look for something you'll feel comfortable wearing. Allow for room to grow."

~Erma Bombeck

Be Compatible

Never have I thought of Dr. Seuss as a philosopher, but he has a quote that I just love. It states, "We are all a little weird and life's a little weird, and when we find someone whose weirdness is compatible with ours, we join up with them and fall in mutual weirdness and call it love."

Men enjoy dating and meeting new women, exploring new interests and having new adventures. Being in a committed relationship leading toward marriage seems very final to them. So when they are looking for a woman of wife material, it is imperative this woman shares common interests about the issues and values they find important. In fact, men get excited when they find someone who is genuinely excited about the same things they are excited about.

My friend Marvin is a 33 year-old financial consultant and actor in New York City. During the performances for an Off, Off Broadway play he was starring in, he met and fell in love with the female lead. There was something in her spirit that grabbed him. However not wanting to mix business with pleasure, he waited until she showed him she shared his romantic interest before pursuing the relationship further. As they dated, he quickly recognized they had a lot in common: they shared the same spiritual beliefs, were college-educated and had similar Caribbean upbringings. As they were both actors, they understood each other's dedication to the craft including all the time and preparation that went into auditioning and rehearsing for roles. Emotions progressed quickly and after only two weeks of dating, they expressed their love for one another. A year after their first date, he proposed to her in the place they held their most sacred common interest…at church. They are now married and looking forward to the beautiful unfolding experiences marriage will bring into their lives.

A high level of trust, respect, honesty, communication and spirituality are the overall values men find important to have in common with their potential wife. They determine if a woman is an individual who shares similar values as their own in many ways including: observing interactions with her friends, family and the general public, politics, religious beliefs, listening to the statements and claims she makes, as well as directly questioning her about the topics of deep interest to them.

Education and intelligence also rank highly as important values to men when looking at a woman as wife material. Although it may not be as important she has the same level of education they possess, men believe someone who is similarly as educated as themselves would have comparable experiences and compatible interests to theirs. By sharing similar interests and values, men feel more confident the relationship will be sustainable long-term.

Keeping all this in mind, it is highly unlikely for a man and woman to have everything in common. A marriage is two distinct individuals coming together. So there are certain values each person will have to adopt in order to create a harmonious relationship. A relationship won't lead to marriage if the attitude is "my way or the highway" on every single aspect. If a couple can uncover several areas of compatibility, and be reasonable on areas where they are not compatible, they will tap into the possibility of a long-term relationship leading to marriage. Even if certain values change throughout the years, the marriage will remain strong.

Wife Material Lesson

Becoming a woman of wife material means you become willing to share your values and interests with your partner. Discovering commonalities reveal compatibility. Your level of compatibility will be conveyed through interactions with friends, family, the general public, as well as the statements and claims you express. Upon determining compatibility, relationships possess a higher level of trust, respect, honesty, intelligence and communication. In addition, harmony is created in your relationship when you appear to be reasonable with your partner even in areas you may not be compatible. Grasping an understanding that certain values and interests may evolve throughout the years, your marriage will strengthen and grow as you allow room for personal growth.

Reflections #7

1. What values and interests do you feel are most important in your life? What about in your marriage?
2. How do you display trust, respect, honesty, intelligence, communication and spirituality in relationships?
3. How important is the education and intelligence of your partner to you? Does it matter if his educational level is higher or lower than yours?
4. How do you handle dissonance in your relationship when you find your partner has a value or interest that's different from yours? How can you be more flexible?
5. If you have a partner, have you asked him what his values and interests are? Are they compatible with your own?

Secret #8
Be Jekyll and Hyde

"A good wife is one who serves her husband in the morning like a mother does, loves him in the day like a sister does and pleases him like a prostitute in the night."

~ Chanakya

Be Jekyll and Hyde

Love was the muse of my 34 year-old girlfriend, Nicole. It would inspire her to write the most beautiful poetry. However, she felt love slipped through her fingers when she and her high school sweetheart divorced after only three and a half years of marriage. She was devastated and wondered if she would ever be able to find love again. She enjoyed being married and wanted to have a family. It felt like her dream of being a wife and mother was taken away from her. That was until a few years later when she reunited with a past flame through a popular social networking site. Passion heated up between them quickly and they were married within months of reconnecting. Having recently given birth to their first child, I asked her what she thought it was about her that attracted her second husband to her. Shockingly, she revealed to me, "I had very few sexual inhibitions when it came to the men I dated and married."

It is common knowledge that men are sexual creatures. They are the reason the Playboy brand name is such a profitable enterprise. Men make strip clubs lucrative and are the motivation for the immense amount of porn that can be found online. But when it comes to their wives, they aren't looking for the video vixen. They want her to be a woman they can introduce to their family and friends. The type of woman with whom they can see themselves starting a family. This type of woman, by most standards, would be considered a lady. But the lady they introduce to their friends is not the same one they want in their bedroom when the lights go out. Thus the popular statement, "Men want a lady in the street and a freak in the bedroom."

Most men when looking for a woman to marry are looking for a woman to be like the main character in the popular novel, the "Strange Case of Dr. Jekyll and Mr. Hyde." She is an upstanding and upright citizen during the daytime but at night she becomes something completely different. There is something a little strange about her, maybe even something slightly sinister. The thought of that is what gets many men to tune into making the woman they are dating their wife.

The reason why most men fear marriage isn't because they fear commitment as much as they fear boredom. The thought of being with the exact same woman every single night makes them cringe compared to the adventure and freedom they have of being with several different women while they are single. It's the idea of variety and spontaneity that turns men on. When a man can sense the woman he's dating will create enough versatility inside and outside the bedroom to keep him intrigued, he will then begin to see her as a woman suitable for settling down.

Wife Material Lesson

As a woman of wife material you become the woman who a man can introduce to his family and friends as well as the type of woman he can see himself starting a family. In addition to this you must also be willing to step out of your comfort zone sexually with your partner. Be open to trying new positions, places and toys to capture the heart of your man. Once he combines your sexual prowess with the fact you are a quality woman who is loving, compatible, and the other six secrets discussed in this book, he will definitely see you as someone he can marry.

Reflections #8

1. On a scale of 1-10 (10- being extremely sexual and 1-being not sexual at all), how sexual would you currently say you are?
2. How do you feel about the statement "Men want a lady in the street and a freak in the bedroom?"
3. How open are you to exploring new positions, places and toys sexually?
4. What can you do to create more variety and spontaneity in the bedroom?
5. What turns you on sexually? If you have a partner, what turns him on?

Secret #9
Be a Good Money Manager

"There's a way of transferring funds that is even faster than electronic banking. It's called marriage."

~ Oscar Wilde

Be a Good Money Manager

It is commonly reported that before Alexander the Great set out to conquer Asia he inquired into the finances of his soldiers. To make sure none of them would worry about the dependents they left behind, he distributed crown estates and revenues among them. As far as Alexander the Great was concerned, it didn't matter if he exhausted all his royal resources. He understood that if his men felt their loved ones were financially taken care of and secure, they would be more focused on successfully completing the mission before them.

Men see marriage the same way. They associate it with great risk. They know that marriage will monetarily affect them. They think about their obligation to pay their partner's bills during a marriage and to provide for their future family. They also fear if the marriage comes to an end, they will be stuck with their partner's bills and have to pay child support and even alimony. Having been taught the financial responsibility of the household is their primary concern; men tend to look for partners who they believe will be more of a financial asset than a liability. This trend was prompted by the Women's Liberation Movement which showed men their standard of living would be increased if there were two bread winners in the household instead of just one. Women went to work so they could gain a feeling of independence and accomplishment. Several decades later, it has now become one of the measuring sticks men use to determine if they will marry a woman.

Every man is different as to how much emphasis he places on his partner's earning potential, but a man wants to know before he marries a woman if she is able to contribute to his financial quality of life in some way. A man will observe the woman to see: Whether she has a job? What type of income she makes? Is she a good financial budgeter? Is she thrifty, or an over spender? Will she keep him from overspending? Does she come from a wealthy family who will leave her a major inheritance? These are the types of questions men ponder as they decide if the woman they are dating has wife potential.

One of the main ways a man discovers how good a money manager a woman is by watching her spending and saving habits. A woman who constantly goes on shopping sprees, makes impulse purchases and maxes out her credit cards is most likely not the type of woman a man will choose as his bride. Neither is the one who doesn't think about her future. Having bad credit, no savings account, investments or 401K makes a man wonder how practical she is.

The inverse of this also rings true. If a woman is a great money manager, it can intimidate men who have not amassed as much. A single woman, who makes a high salary, owns her own home, has a large savings account, perfect credit, 401K plan and is a great budgeter can make many men feel financially insecure. If a man sees he doesn't have anything to contribute, he won't think he has enough to offer her. To get around this, the woman has to focus more on using words like "us" and "ours" instead of "I" and "mine." If the man resonates with her success, it will also make him feel successful. Creating this space gives him the self-confidence essential to believing he's contributing to the relationship.

Regardless of who is making the most money in the relationship, men also view fairness in deciding to marry a woman. Is the woman always looking for him to pay for the dates or does she pay for dates as well? Does she only receive gifts and surprises from him, or does she reciprocate by doing the same? If he is having hard times, is she willing to assist him financially until he's back on his feet, or will she turn her back on him? The answers to these questions will aid him in deciding the seriousness the relationship.

Wife Material Lesson

As a woman of wife material you know men see marriage as a major financial risk so you assist your partner in feeling secure by becoming a good money manager. Displaying your earning potential, maintaining moderate spending habits, and becoming a good financial budgeter will get him to tune into you. He will also be encouraged to view you as more of an asset to the relationship if you show you are fiscally fair. This can be displayed in various ways such as paying for dates and taking care of your partner. Regardless of who makes more money in the relationship, you encourage your partner to feel like he is a successful contributor, which will draw him closer to you and allow him to see you as wife potential.

Reflections #9

1. How are you able to financially contribute to a relationship?
2. Do you have good spending and saving habits? If not, what can you do to improve them?
3. Have you ever felt you intimidated a man because you were such a good money manager? If so, what do you feel you can you do to overcome this?
4. Are you financially fair in relationships? If not, how can you improve?
5. In what ways can you increase your money management skills?

Secret #10
Be Supportive

"The real act of marriage takes place in the heart, not in the ballroom or church or synagogue. It's a choice you make - not just on your wedding day, but over and over again - and that choice is reflected in the way you treat your husband or wife."

~Barbara de Angelis

Be Supportive

There was a story I once read about a military veteran named Master Sgt. Jeffrey Mittman who was severely wounded by a roadside bomb during the Iraqi war in Baghdad. His face had been totally disfigured. He lost his nose, lips as well as most of his teeth and his left eye was damaged causing him to be blind.

While in rehabilitation, his biggest concern was for his family. How would he be able to recover and take care of them? During this time, his wife was his biggest supporter. She remained by his side throughout his lengthy recovery process and once he was discharged she encouraged him to go back to school and get his Master's degree in Executive Development for Public Service and eventually a second Master's degree in Business Administration. Now an inspirational public speaker and a national account manager with the National Industries for the Blind, he credits his wife for his amazing progress saying, "I'm where I am today because of my wife, Christy."

Nothing in life is guaranteed. This is one of the biggest fears that ring true to men when it comes to getting married. They realize they only have limited control over their future, especially when someone else is involved. Being unable to predict the trials and tribulations of life makes them uncomfortable. So when looking for a life partner, they aren't looking for a fair-weather female. They are looking for someone who will take the vows, "for better or for worst" seriously. Someone who they trust will support them during both good and bad times.

A supportive woman increases her partner's motivation in becoming a better man. She ignites within him a sense of his best self, which is what men really want. She believes in his dreams and encourages him to push beyond his limitations to achieve his goals toward the life he envisions. She challenges him to become the man he truly wants to be.

There is power in being a supportive woman. Her support draws her mate into her. For example, let's say she wants her partner to be healthier. She may simply remind him of his desire to be healthy and support him in that goal. By making him healthier meals at home, working out with him at the gym, or joining him for a jog around the block, she is actively showing him her support.

Because so often, women are not supportive, this one trait alone really makes a woman stand out to a man. Knowing she will be there for him regardless of the circumstances will only enhance his self-confidence as well as his assurance in her. Thus increasing his belief she could be a good life partner.

Wife Material Lesson

As a woman of wife material you become supportive of your partner because you know your motivation and encouragement will help him attain his goals. You begin to understand when a man is looking for a life partner; he is looking for a woman who he can trust to take the vow "for better or for worst" seriously. Therefore, you become a sound woman who will be by his side during the uncertain times and inspire him when times are good. You will challenge him to push beyond his limitations to be the man he always envisioned himself to be. Thus you will become the type of woman he will consider making his wife.

Reflections #10

1. Are you a supportive person? Can you see yourself supporting your partner through both good and bad times?

2. How do you like to be motivated and supported? If you have a partner how does he like to be motivated and supported?

3. In what ways are you encouraging? If you have a partner, how are you encouraging his dreams and goals? How is he encouraging yours?

4. If you have a partner, what area would you like to encourage him that would also be of benefit to you?

5. What can you do to become a more supportive person in your relationships?

5 Most Common Obstacles to Overcome to
Get A Ring On It

"The difference between a successful person and others is not a lack of strength, not a lack of knowledge, but rather a lack of determination."

~ Vince Lombardi

5 Most Common Obstacles To Overcome To
Get A Ring On It

Congrats! Now you are aware of the *10 Secrets to Becoming Wife Material.* However, the success you will gain from the knowledge of these secrets will be limited unless you are able to first overcome the obstacles that have separated you from already having been married. It begins and ends with you. You are the common denominator. You are the person who chose every person you dated (or didn't date) and created your current relationship circumstance. The good news is, upon acknowledgement and understanding of this; you are also the one who can choose a different path and attract the committed, romantic love you desire.

It has been stated, "Love is a journey, not a destination." During the journey, you may have grasped certain thoughts, habits and behaviors that no longer serve you in attracting a husband. It is important to release this emotional baggage. This is because it is impossible to focus on both the absence of love and attainment of love at the same time. From my research, I will share with you the 5 most common obstacles to overcome so you may *Get A Ring On It*. Making these simple mental shifts will create the breakthrough you have been craving in your love life.

Determine which of the following obstacles have been keeping you from your heart's desire. Continuing to hold on to the emotional baggage, will keep you longing to one day be a wife. Release this baggage and it will only be a matter of time before you *Get A Ring On It*.

Obstacle #1: Lack of Clearly Defined Love Goal and Plan

Have you ever been successful when you didn't have a clearly defined goal? You most likely had a goal and plans for every important aspect of your life including school and your career. So why is it you left one of the most influential areas of your life to chance? Did you expect love to magically show up in your life with little to no research or planning? Your life is not a Disney movie. In reality, it is important to treat your love life like every other important aspect of your life. Define what it is you truly want. Then create a plan to attain it. The plan can be revised over time, but your love goal should be S.M.A.R.T: Specific, Measurable, Attainable, Realistic and Time. It is possible you may have to change certain habits, thoughts or behaviors in order to achieve your outcome. Enhance those traits that encourage a harmonious relationship. Also, get a handle on what you can contribute to a partnership as well as what could discourage a lasting relationship. Establishing a clearly defined love goal and plan will provide the foundation for attaining a long-lasting commitment.

Obstacle #2: Negative Mental Attitude

Have you ever heard the phrase, "If you think you can, you can. If you think you can't, you can't?" This quote, attributed to Henry Ford, goes on to explain, "Either way, you are right." Does this give you a glimpse into the power of having a positive mental attitude? It has been proven that those who think positively on a situation are more likely to get the outcome they aspire to than those who don't. If you don't believe you can meet a man who you love, who will want to commit and marry you, then chances are no matter how well you implement the 10 Secrets shared within this book, you will not attract and sustain a healthy romantic relationship. With what type of attitude are you approaching your love life? Are you approaching it with positive expectancy, optimism and enthusiasm? Or are you approaching it with pessimism, hopelessness and despair? Either way, you are right.

Obstacle #3: Unresolved Issues

One of the biggest challenges in intimate relationships, is the fact many people enter them in order to complete an aspect of themselves. They seek to attract people who have the attributes they are missing. These may be considered unresolved issues. If they are poor, they want someone who is rich. If they are un-educated, they want someone who has an education. If they are shy, they want someone who is outgoing. Yes, opposites can attract. However, these types of relationships seldom last long-term. This may be because these relationships become more about receiving than giving. The partnerships become based more on dependency than being complimentary.

Another place unresolved issues might appear is in what angers you in a romantic partner. Of course, no one deliberately makes contact with someone who is dishonest, disloyal or unhealthy. However, if these characteristics are revealing themselves in the men you date, the question you may want to ask yourself is: where are these traits showing up in areas of your own life? For example, if you want someone who will see your value, feel if you value yourself? If not, what ways can you decide to elevate your value?

The truth of the matter is we tend to attract who we are. Distinct issues that irritate us are usually unhealed aspects of unresolved issues or ourselves. Who we date and what they present to us is often a reflection of who we are. Instead of challenging someone else to have the traits you are looking for, it would be more desirable for you to develop those attributes within yourself. Resolving any unsound issues within you will be the best way to attract a healthy, loving relationship and marriage.

Obstacle #4: Excuses and Limiting Beliefs

Have you ever thought about why you aren't currently married? I mean really thought about it? Chances are you have several justifiable and unjustifiable excuses and limiting beliefs that have created your circumstance. To assist you in uncovering which convictions influenced your fate, I want to share 50 common reasons why women believe they are not married. Which one of these statements resonates with you?

1. I am too focused on my career.
2. My standards are too high (or too low).
3. I can't afford to get married.
4. I don't want to change my last name.
5. I am waiting until all people are able to marry.
6. I don't need a symbolic public ceremony to legalize something I already have.
7. I already have a "gay husband," I don't need an actual husband.
8. I simply don't want to be married.
9. I don't believe in monogamy (or all men cheat).

10. I already get enough sex (or am not a sexual person).
11. I have "issues."
12. I don't need a man for financial security (or need a man who is wealthy).
13. Men of my race only date women of other races.
14. I have enough male friends; I don't need a husband.
15. I am a single parent.
16. I just got out of a serious relationship.
17. I recently got divorced.
18. I don't think I'm good enough to be married.
19. I can't find a quality man (or there are no quality men where I live).
20. I have too much emotional baggage.
21. I don't believe marriage still works.
22. My parent's divorce still bothers me.
23. I don't know how to identify a good man.
24. I intimidate men.
25. I believe all the good men are gay or in jail.
26. I think men have too many dating options.
27. I don't believe I can "have it all": Career and marriage.
28. I think I'm too independent for marriage (or I don't want to lose my independence).
29. I have never seen a good marriage.
30. I am dating a man who doesn't believe in marriage.
31. I don't want to take on the responsibility of being a wife.

32. I don't want to add stress to my current relationship or myself.
33. I am afraid of the idea of being married.
34. I have bad timing when it comes to relationships.
35. I have a fear of commitment.
36. I fear marriage will change my life dramatically.
37. I think I am too high maintenance.
38. I think I am too fat to attract a husband (or too skinny).
39. I am too busy to date or get married.
40. I only meet men who are players.
41. I don't know how to meet men.
42. I do not know how to cook.
43. I believe I am too old to be married (or too young).
44. I am dating someone who is already in a committed relationship with someone else.
45. I don't like online dating (or dating in general).
46. I don't believe men know how to be chivalrous anymore.
47. I haven't been able to attract a man who will commit to me.
48. I can only meet potential marital partners through family or friends.
49. I already had my one great love, and since that didn't work out I don't believe I'll ever find another.
50. I refuse to enter into a lifetime contract with someone with whom I'm not 100% sure I want to marry.

Did any of the above statements ring a bell? If you go back and re-examine these declarations, you will realize they are all simply doubts, fears, worries and insecurities in disguise. Who determined any of these statements as true? You did. Limitations are self-imposed. The same way you were once able to see them as true, you can now choose to view them as excuses and limiting beliefs. Women are getting married every day. Many of these women even had situations similar to that described above. However, those reasons were not sufficient enough to prevent them from attaining their goal of marriage. Why should it restrain you? Stop thinking of all the reasons why you can't get married. Instead focus on all the reasons you can. Releasing these excuses and limiting beliefs will give you the freedom to believe you can attract marriage into your life and forever change the circumstances around you to harmonize with your goal.

Obstacle #5: Indifference and Inaction

In Physics class you may have remembered learning, Issac Newton's First Law of Motion. It is often stated as, "An object at rest stays at rest, and an object in motion stays in motion." You say you want to get married but are you in motion? What activities are you executing each day to make your love goal a reality? The reason many women remain single is because they spend more time wishing they were in a relationship than they do actually doing something about it. Don't be one of these women.

It's important for you to place yourself in the positions where you can meet someone who could potentially become your husband. Today there are more outlets than ever before to socially connect and meet someone. Don't let your love life pass you by. Get into the driver's seat, and drive that baby all the way to your love destination!

Know there are no circumstances adequate enough to prevent you from being able to *Get A Ring On It*. All you need is purpose, perseverance and faith. In the words of Charles Kettering "Believe and act as if it were impossible to fail."

Reflections #11

1. Clearly define your love goal as a S.M.A.R.T. goal. What is your plan to achieve this goal?

2. Create a positive image of yourself being in the healthy, romantic marriage you desire. This can be written as a description, poem, song or illustration.

3. List the qualities you are looking for in your life partner. Also list the qualities that anger you when thinking about a life partner. Do you notice any unresolved issues in yourself? What steps can you take to heal them?

4. Circle or highlight any of the 50 common reasons women believe they are not married which in the past created your current relationship status.

5. What actions can you initiate today to work toward your love goal?

Conclusion

After everything we hear about the uncertainty of marriage: increasing divorce rates, people changing and financial losses why do we still long to be married? I believe it's because we yearn to explore the deep romantic connection of love through a lifetime commitment and partnership. Marriage is still viewed by our society as the highest institution of exclusivity a man and woman can attain.

The challenge most single women face is we have not taken adequate time to understand marriage from the man's point of view or ourselves. Many times as women we remain single because we don't always know what men are looking for in a wife. We see the man's confidence, but not his fears, doubts and insecurities that lay underneath.

Upon uncovering the *10 Secrets To Becoming Wife Material*, we now realize men are people too. What men are looking for in a wife are the same things we are looking for in a husband: love, fidelity and security. It is important for us to take this under consideration because men are traditionally the ones who ask for our hand in marriage, not the other way around. Therefore as women wanting to be married, it's important for us to tune into what men are looking for in a wife so we may be viewed as wife material.

Men want to be married. They aspire to find a partner with whom they can share their lives. They want to have children within the bonds of marriage. However, they realize it will be one of the most important decisions they make in their lives. They proceed cautiously knowing it will have a major affect on them personally, physically, emotionally and financially. Therefore, they logically take a look at all the risks and try to find a woman who can minimize their fears, doubts and insecurities. Once they have found a woman who possesses the characteristics and traits they are looking for, they become confident in their decision and are willing to accept the risk.

When Josh, a newly engaged 28 year-old graduate student, was asked in a focus group what made him decide to propose, he passionately revealed, "Marriage is important to me. I found someone who would work with me in this constantly changing world and would be my partner. I want to publicly declare to her, her family and myself that I am in this relationship for the long haul and put a label on it. I feel this is important to our family, friends and other people that care about us. The wedding ceremony will be a symbol of our long-term commitment to each other. Based on what I know about her, I believe this is the best decision for us and this gives me peace of mind."

Knowing the *10 Secrets To Becoming Wife Material* will separate you from the vast majority of single women who want to be married. These secrets will give you confidence and assure you are on the right track, to making a man feel at ease around you, and want to secure a lifelong commitment with you. He will be able to see the qualities and characteristics in you he desires in a life partner and it will not be long until you go from being wife material to someone's wife.

Once a wife, maintaining these secrets will serve you well in creating a harmonious, loving and sustainable marriage. It's not about simply getting married, but staying committed in the marriage. Continuing to stay wife material throughout the marriage will make it less likely you'll become divorced and single again. Therefore, continue practicing these secrets even after you *Get A Ring On It*.

Discussion Questions

*Further questions for you to ask yourself
or discuss in your book club*

1. Which of these 10 secrets do you feel you already possess?
2. Which of these 10 secrets will be the most challenging for you to add to your life? Why?
3. How would you describe a woman who is wife material after reading this book?
4. What behaviors do you need to enhance, modify or supplement to your dating practices so you can go from being single to wife material?
5. What did you learn from this book about men that surprised you most? What concepts resonated the most with you about men?
6. Do you feel what men are looking for in a life-long partner is different than what women are looking for? If so, what do you think is the difference?

7. Has the Women's Liberation Movement helped or hindered women's romantic lives?

8. What is your vision of the ideal husband?

9. What do you believe is an ideal marriage?

10. How will knowing these 10 secrets better prepare you while dating and during marriage?

About The Author

Lasana Smith is a vivacious dating and relationship expert and media personality who has been featured in The Huffington Post, MSNBC.com, Nerve.com and the popular Yahoo! Web-series, "Let's Talk About Love" with Niecy Nash. She contributed her knowledge and expertise as a featured writer for the Tyra Banks show online magazine's "Single and Fierce" section and currently writes her own relationship blog, LoveandLifeblog.com. She spent over a year researching and conducting focus groups with men and women to gain a better understanding of the question, "Is The Single, Modern Woman Having A Difficult Time Finding A Husband?" for her Master's thesis in Communication Management at the University of Southern California. Lasana Smith's first book on Dating and Relationships is, "*Get A Ring On It: 10 Secrets To Becoming Wife Material.*"

For the latest updates on Lasana Smith:

- ★ Website:www.lasanaonline.com
- ★ Blog: www.loveandlifeblog.com
- ★ YouTube:youtube.com/lasanaonline
- ★ Tweet:@Lasana and @LoveandLifeblog
- ★ Be a Fan: facebook.com/lasanaonline

www.ingramcontent.com/pod-product-compliance
Lightning Source LLC
LaVergne TN
LVHW051505070426
835507LV00022B/2930